LET'S GET FOCUSED

SUGGESTIONS FOR IMPROVING AMERICA

RONALD F. JACKSON

LET'S GET
FOCUSED

RONALD F. JACKSON

Copyright © 2025 by Ronald F. Jackson

All rights reserved. No part of this publication may be reproduced, distributed, or transmitted in any form or by any means, including photocopying, recording, or other electronic or mechanical methods, without the prior written permission of the copyright owner and the publisher, except in the case of brief quotations embodied in critical reviews and certain other noncommercial uses permitted by copyright law. For permission requests, write to the publisher, addressed "Attention: Permissions Coordinator," at the address below.

CITIOFBOOKS, INC.
3736 Eubank NE Suite A1
Albuquerque, NM 87111-3579
www.citiofbooks.com
 Hotline: 1 (877) 389-2759
 Fax: 1 (505) 930-7244

Ordering Information:
Quantity sales. Special discounts are available on quantity purchases by corporations, associations, and others. For details, contact the publisher at the address above.

Printed in the United States of America.

ISBN-13:	Softcover	979-8-89391-863-2
	eBook	979-8-89391-865-6
	Hardback	979-8-89391-864-9

Library of Congress Control Number: 2025917228

Contents

INTRODUCTION i

PART 1 1
   1. Second Amendment Revision 2
   2. Term Limits 4
   3. Voting Rights 5
   4. Elections 6
   5. Gerrymandering 7
   6. Personhood 8
   7. Political Discourse 8
   8. Presidential Elections 9
   9. National Referendum 12
   10. Senate Reform 13
   11. Reproductive Rights 14

PART TWO 15
   1. Taxes and Economy 15
   2. Social Security and Medicare 18
   3. Immigration 21
   4. Social Justice and Judicial Reform 22
   5. Internet and Social Media 24
   6. Usury 25
   7. National Oil Company 26
   8. The Filibuster, Nominations and Appointments 26
   9. Schools 27
   10. Decriminalize Drug Use 29
   11. Ethics in Politics and the Judiciary 30

INTRODUCTION

After all other possibilities have been exhausted, Americans will do the right thing. That was the British view during World War II. We have not changed much. Americans are quite stubborn and do not like to be told what to do even if it is in their best interests. We are also politically lazy and tend to leave things to the sometimes idiots we put in office. We allow sloppy and sometimes corrupt media work to sway us instead of doing our own research and seeking the truth for ourselves. Additionally, we have the attention span of earthworms and that's an insult to earthworms. Despite that, this book is being offered in the hopes that it will stimulate some discussion and action that moves the country to a better place and allows it to work for that "more perfect union" rather than just talk about it while blindly stuck in the traditions of the past. Progress and movement do risk mistakes. So, if a mistake is made, man up, fess up and fix it. We should not be afraid or averse to change for fear of making a mistake. Just like a marriage, democracy takes work. If you neglect either a marriage or democracy, they will fall apart. In that light, what follows are several proposals which would, if implemented advance American society and get us closer to that "more perfect union". The proposals are divided into subjects that are vital for going forward and therefore rising to the level of Constitutional Amendments. Other proposals are laws, policies or problem-solving approaches that would be beneficial too. This book is short and succinct. No attempt to spend much time recounting history or examples of how others have changed their societies is made. The attempt is to stay focused on issues and potential solutions. Read, discuss, and enjoy.

PART 1

The United States constitution was written in 1787 and ratified in 1788. This book is being written in 2023. That is over 240 years, and it is time to assess strengths and weaknesses with the perspective of time and experience. For those who believe the constitution was "divinely inspired" please know that that makes as much sense as seeing little green men after a night of heavy drinking. If you do not believe it study the Romans and you will be shocked at the parallels in the systems of government. Polybius, Tacitus, and Dio are some references to support this claim. The founders had classical education. When looking around for a government to model on, they had the monarchy, which they wanted no part of, or they could model the most successful government in history, Rome. On a purely common-sense level, do we really think we have learned nothing since 1787 or that we do not have the reason to see problems and propose solutions. Was the pinnacle of human thought and reasoning 1787 such that modern society has nothing to contribute to the progress of humanity or the goal of securing a 'more perfect union". To believe this is lazy and unworthy of the freedoms we have been fortunate enough to be heirs to. "A republic if you can keep it," was Benjamin Franklin's answer to the type of government the founders had provided. Well keeping it requires work. Work that makes the system better for all not some perverted manipulation that secures power and profit for a few at the expense of others. A review of Roman history again would provide some warnings about greed and lust for power at the expense of the common good. We live in a multicultural, multi-ethnic nation and one could argue that makes our task even more difficult. It is all too easy to look at" the other" and not see them as worthy of the same benefits as you enjoy or dismiss another's mistreatment and suffering because after all, it's not me or mine why should I get involved? How does the old quote go, "the only thing necessary for the triumph of evil is for good men to do nothing"? Well, it is time we grew up, took responsibility for our wellbeing, and assumed the mantle of leadership. I am not saying the constitution should be whimsically altered with every passing fade. I do think it should be a slow and difficult process. But we have stymied ourselves from even trying or thinking seriously about updating our founding document. Because it is difficult is no excuse for not trying. Because it is time consuming patience and perseverance must be exercised. So, grow up America, let's get started!

Below are 11 changes to the constitution that would help address some of the more difficult problems the country faces as well as some updates more appropriate for the modern world.

Constitutional Changes

1. Second Amendment Revision

Citizens of the United States are permitted to own and possess weapons subject to the restrictions and requirements imposed by federal, State and/or local jurisdictions, as deemed necessary by said federal, State and/or local jurisdiction, to maintain safety and order.

Context and common sense. That is what is missing in the discussion of guns in this country. The Second Amendment to the United States Constitution was adopted on December 15, 1791, along with nine other amendments comprising the Bill of Rights. The Second Amendment protects the right of individuals to keep and bear arms. The second amendment reads, "A well-regulated Militia, being necessary to the security of a free State, the right of the people to keep and bear Arms, shall not be infringed." The founders were vehemently opposed to a standing army and did not provide for one at the founding of the country. This is understandable since they had witnessed the English standing army abusing Americans and fighting a war against them. The amendment was added to the Constitution in response to the concern that a national standing army posed a threat to individual liberty and that the federal government might disarm the state militias, which were considered essential for the defense of a free state. The exact rationale behind the amendment is a matter of ongoing debate and interpretation. Some argue that it was intended to ensure the right of citizens to form a militia to protect themselves against a tyrannical government, while others argue that it was intended to ensure the right of citizens to use firearms for hunting and self-defense.

But there was the very real possibility the country would be attacked by a foreign power, and it would be necessary to mount a defense. The British were just over the border in Canada, and it was possible they would come back, as they did in the War of 1812. Since there was no standing army and no armory full of weapons that could be drawn on when needed, any citizen serving in the defense of the nation needed to bring his own weapon. Another Roman parallel, in the early days of their republic soldiers provided their own equipment and there was no standing army. Armies were raised to meet specific threats by wealthy Senators. Fast forward to today and the disdain for a standing military has long since been discarded and there is no need for recruits to show up with their own weapons. That is what that first line of the second amendment is all about, you know that part WHICH always gets ignored. Given the weaponry and might of the U.S. military, this fanciful idea that individual citizens can prevail against the government is as anachronistic as butter churns. The only way to reverse this is to allow individuals to be armed with any weapon available to the military. While this may appeal to some fringe elements, I don't think most people would relish the idea of their neighbor having a nuclear bomb on the wall over his fireplace. No, it's time we accepted the fact that the way we change our government is by voting. If you don't like what the government is doing, then vote new people into office that will implement the policies you want.

So, in keeping with that context, placing requirements on ownership as well as restricting some kinds of weapons the founders could not have imagined in their wildest dreams does not seem like a violation that foils the intent of the second amendment. Reasonable public safety requirements should be something we can all live with. If Wyoming wants to allow open carry, fine. But I think New Yorkers would feel differently about arming ten million of their neighbors. So, let us use a little common sense and tailor regulations to the local community. Needless to say, weapons traversing state lines from areas where they are allowed to those that restrict them must be monitored and strictly controlled.

2. Term Limits

Senators are allowed to serve for 18 years (3, 6-year terms); members of the House of Representatives are allowed to serve 18 years (9, 2-year terms); federal judges and supreme court justices are allowed to serve one 20-year term and must be at least 50 years of age; and must have spent at least three years each as a prosecutor and a defense attorney and must be approved by 3/5 of the Senate.

The Founding Fathers did not include term limits for federal positions like senators, judges, and congressmen in the Constitution because they believed in the idea of "citizen legislators." They thought that elected officials should be regular citizens who temporarily serve in government and then return to private life. They believed that elected officials who were not professional politicians would be less likely to become corrupt and more likely to be in touch with the needs and concerns of the people.

Additionally, they believed that elected officials who were not limited by term limits would be able to gain experience and expertise in their positions, which would make them more effective in serving the country.

Career politicians lose contact with the public and cease serving the people in favor of seeking re-election. On the other hand, people with experience at their jobs do develop competence over time. It is of great value to have political leadership in place that has seen various cycles, war and peace, economic boom and bust, etc. New blood and fresh ideas are needed throughout society and most of all in the political arena. Staying in office too long doesn't bring office holders closer to the general public. On the contrary they become Patricians, part of a protected class, untouchables whose thoughts and ideas are the only ones with merit. Term limits will break the hold of incompetent or corrupt politicians on the office they hold. Eighteen years is enough time for senators and congressmen to gain broad experience and be proficient at making government work while not blocking new talent or entrenching mediocrity or corruption. Those desiring to remain in government service can always seek another office and serve 18 years in that position.

Similarly, judges should not be so entrenched that they lose contact with the rest of the population and normal daily life. Rotating judges out after a fixed term will ensure fresh blood and perspectives are brought to the bench that reflect the mood of the population. Age requirements are imposed on judges in the hope that candidates have had broad life experience with all its ups, downs, successes, and failures. Age requirements do not ensure humility and a broad perspective, but it is a step in that direction. The requirement to have both prosecutor and defense attorney experience is to ensure broad experience and true understanding of how the justice system works. One can sympathize with the fox while appreciating the perspective of the hound. Finally, if anything needs broad consensus and agreement it should be judges. First, they should be competent, compassionate, and centrist. They should not be ideologs groomed and paid for by partisan groups seeking to manipulate the judiciary. It's no secret malleable law students are identified during their studies and introduced to various groups and points of view to develop potential candidates for the judiciary. The most promising are given the best job opportunities, clerkship's and may have student loans or mortgages paid. When people know how a judge will rule prior to a case being heard, courts have no validity. Let's put a stop to gaming the system.

3. Voting Rights

The right to vote shall not be hindered or encumbered in any way. All United States citizens shall be automatically registered to vote at 18 years of age. Incarcerated persons may have voting privileges suspended during the incarceration period but voting rights must be restored at the completion of incarceration. Where identification is required, it must be provided free of charge to U. S. citizens and must be physically available at locations no more than 25 miles from cities and county seats. No citizen shall wait more than 30 minutes to vote when presenting themselves in person. No U. S. citizen shall be disenfranchised because of process or procedural anomalies or issues.

The Voting Rights Act was passed in 1965 and here we are in 2023 facing a constant assault on and erosion of those rights. Make no mistake, nothing is being protected. This is a naked power grab based on demographic fear of non-whites being a voting majority in this country. Some people simply cannot imagine sharing power with others that don't look like them and who may have very different views on how things should be done. Voting rights really comes down to who we really are and what we believe. Do we really think all men are created equal? Do we believe in fairness and justice? If we do everyone should have the same opportunity to vote and their votes should count equally. In 2023 we have surely had enough elections to understand the relationship between the number of voters in a precinct, the number of poll workers and the number of voting machines and their affect on wait times. Expend the resources necessary to get wait times down to 30 minutes maximum across the country. Identification should never impede citizens from voting. Various methods should be used to identify citizens such as drivers' licenses, student IDs, utility bills, voter ID cards etc. Similarly, cost should not impede voting when an ID is required.

4. Elections

Elections shall be in person and absentee by mail and/or online. Voting in elections shall be continuous for 30 days prior to the final election deadline. Election disputes shall be settled in courts of law using the rules of evidence, the truth and fairness. Election results shall be available within 5 hours of polls closing.

What is done to voters in this country is a disgrace. We should be making it as easy as possible to participate in the electoral process and we should be doing everything we can to increase voter participation in the process. Expanding the voting period with early voting will allow people to participate regardless of circumstances. The 2020 presidential election had the greatest participation in the country's history. This was because of expanded voting by mail during the COVID – 19 pandemic. We know this works and is safe. Ballots should be returned by mail or in person at collection locations dispersed to have one for every 5000 in population.

Disputes in elections need to be settled by courts following the law with impartiality and fairness. Disputes settled by legislative bodies that are partisan have no credibility and provide a path for unscrupulous people to manipulate the system and thwart the will of the majority.

In 2023, with all the technology available, it should be possible to push a button and know election results in 15 minutes. This is not the case because we are stuck on stupid. Some states refuse to change their processes because that is the way they have always done it. Some states have no early voting. Some states do not allow election workers to start counting and processing absentee ballots until the polls have closed. It's no wonder it takes some states a week to figure out election results. This is foolish and lends itself to doubt and allegations of fraud. It is time to clean it up and get all states into the modern era.

5. *Gerrymandering*

Congressional districts shall be created without consideration of the political leanings, race, creed, color, or religion of the voters involved. Districts shall be contiguous, organized around common issues or interests, have similar shapes, and be bounded by natural or man-made demarcations such as mountains, rivers, city limits, county lines, expressways, etc. Non-partisan commissions shall determine district boundaries.

Voters should pick the politicians they want. The politicians should not pick their voters. This is simple but obvious and we let the professional politicians and power seekers divide us into sides where ideas and common sense do not matter only that one's team wins. If districts are constructed around common interests the population of that district will be better served by people who focus on these issues and develop expertise in addressing them. Where population allows, cities and counties should remain intact because those entities are clearly the largest drivers for that region. Coastal areas should be grouped to address the special needs presented by beach erosion, sea impingement and tourism needs. These are just a couple of examples where common interests can be better served when focused attention is given to them. It makes no sense to group a large urban area with a rural community separated by many miles. The issues and problems are different for each, and both deserve representation that not only intellectually understands the issues but one who also lives with the issues day to day. Think how much better governance could be if the representatives were personally invested and had to appeal to a diverse group of constituents that shared the same problems. We need to move away from tribalism and start embracing our neighbors. This would also lead to less extremism in our politics since the elected representatives will need to appeal to a cross section of voters with diverse opinions.

6. Personhood

Only living human beings post birth are entitled to personhood rights. Legal entities such as corporations, partnerships, etc. have no such rights e.g., free speech, religion, etc.

Plutocracy is a form of power structure in which the elite or ruling class derives its power from wealth. Many want to use corporations to control the country and thwart the will of most of the people. It is the same old story. The wealthy find new and ever more creative ways to maintain power and control. Allowing free speech rights to legal entities puts ordinary citizens at a distinct disadvantage when it comes to resources and influence. Eventually, private entities will desire more influence and something equivalent to a vote. This movement seeks to concentrate power in the hands of a few. Corporations and partnerships are legal constructs designed to formalize how business is conducted, limit liability and reduce taxes. These entities are not people, and it should be very clear that they should not be treated as people at the expense of real citizens. The grooming of judges is ultimately leading to an attempt to get personhood status for corporations and other entities so that their will can have constitutional protection. The dangers of such an event should be obvious.

7. Political Discourse

Political contributions are limited to the federal poverty income limit for a family of four. Only living persons may contribute to political campaigns using personal funds. Third party groups may only advertise to promote or oppose issues and must clearly identify themselves as responsible and make available the identities of all founders, directors, officers, and managers as well as membership of the group. Attacks on candidate by third parties are not permitted.

The love of money is the root of all evil or, so it is said. Does anyone really think people donate hundreds of thousands of dollars to political campaigns and expect nothing in return? Or that candidates do not feel obligated to satisfy their donors? That is contrary to all we know about human nature and all its frailties. If anything can be corrupted men will find a way to do it. Limiting money in politics will go a long way toward limiting the purchase of influence in politics. Limiting contributions will decrease the money that can be raised for a campaign and make running for office more likely for ordinary people who are not wealthy or well connected.

Advertising is the most powerful tool a candidate has to get his message across. That can be overwhelmed by massive ad campaigns mounted by a myriad of dark money groups who have seemingly unlimited money. In most cases who is behind the ads cannot even be discerned. The public has a right to know in detail, who is behind an ad so that they can assess motivation and potentially the veracity of the ad. Sunlight they say is the greatest disinfectant. Full public disclosure allows citizens to determine if they want to align themselves with ad proponents.

8. Presidential Elections

The Electoral College is abolished. Presidents and Vice Presidents shall be elected by the direct vote of the people. Tie elections shall be rerun 45 days after the previous election until a winner is produced. The President-elect will take office 45 days after election.

This is the most obvious change of all. If anyone were setting up a democratic form of government today, they would not opt for an electoral college system. They would opt for a direct vote of the people to be governed. We choose every other office by the direct vote of the people. This includes everything from dog catcher to mayor, congressman, and senator. Indeed, almost all countries that used an electoral system have abolished it in favor of the direct vote. Why do we have this system you say? Look to our old friends the romans once again. Everybody knows about the roman senate, but they also had public assemblies that passed laws. Of course, the wealthy romans were not going to allow ordinary uneducated citizens to dominate politics, so they devised a system where the votes of the wealthy in fact carried more weight than those of ordinary citizens. In fact, they skewed the system such that the votes of older citizens were weighted higher than young people and since the groupings of citizens voted in order, it was possible to pass or defeat a measure with just the votes of the wealthy and ordinary citizens would not even get a chance to vote. Our electoral college system was set up to help big and small states feel more equal, but I think in the modern era most people want all citizens to be equal and do not see the need to operate on a state-by-state basis. We always talk about bringing the country together, yet we perpetuate a system that divides us by state as if Americans in one state are completely alien to those of another state. True democracy demands that our institutions are as democratic as possible. There is no way a system that allows the person with fewer votes to be declared the winner. That is the definition of undemocratic. Since the year 2000 this anomaly has occurred twice. The possibility has many voters disillusioned and feeling that their vote doesn't count. The country literally may not hold together if this should happen again. The "winner" is immediately dubbed illegitimate by supporters of the person getting the most votes. That taint is never removed in the minds of the majority of voters and adds to disfunction and division. For unity's sake we should embrace a clearly fair and democratic system.

The election of 2020 exposed a glaring flaw in our current system for electing presidents. That flaw is that it can be manipulated by unscrupulous people over the will of the majority of voters. What some Republicans tried in 2020 while despicable and antidemocratic, was quite clever and had it been successful would have been within the rules of the game. They had two paths to success and but for a few people with integrity, and I mean a very few, that election could have been reversed despite the winner getting over seven million votes more than the loser. The first path was to sow enough confusion and disinformation(lies) about the election such that governors in battleground states would declare the state election void because of ballot fraud and confusion. They would then declare that the state legislature should pick the state's electors. With most of these legislatures in the hands of Republicans, of course the Republican electors would be chosen. The second path to victory was similar but only required that the battleground states simply throw up their hands and make no decision. The state officials couldn't be accused of doing anything wrong because they were simply saying there is too much confusion, and we can't make a decision. At that point it would be up to the US House of Representatives to determine a winner. The problem is that the decision would not be based on proportional representation which absent gerrymandering might represent the wishes of the people. No, the House vote would be skewed and each state would get one vote. So, California with almost 40 million people would get one vote as would Wyoming with less than 600,000 people. Since Republicans control more state congressional delegations, although they represent fewer voters, Republicans would have won. Let me be clear, the only democratic and legitimate way to elect a president is for people to give that candidate the majority of the votes cast in the election. No legislator either state or federal should be involved with selecting the president other than by casting their ballot at the polls like every other citizen. The path is there. It's staring us in the face and will not go away. It is just a matter of time before another group of usurpers maybe better organized and funded, smarter, more devious, and more determined tries this again. We need to eliminate this weakness before a catastrophe occurs from which the nation cannot recover.

While getting this amendment passed is a daunting task, some very clever people have come up with a way to effectively get the same result without the amendment. The movement is called the National Popular Vote Interstate Compact. The concept is simple. The courts have already determined that states alone may determine how their electoral votes are counted. Most states are winner take all but some states award electoral votes based on who wins a congressional district.

The National Popular Vote Interstate Compact will guarantee the Presidency to the candidate who receives the most popular votes across all 50 states and the District of Columbia. The Compact ensures that *every* vote, in *every* state, will matter in *every* presidential election. The Compact is a state-based approach that preserves the Electoral College, state control of elections, and the power of the states to control how the President is elected.

The National Popular Vote bill has been enacted by 17 jurisdictions possessing 205 electoral votes, including 4 small states (DE, HI, RI, VT), 9 medium-sized states (CO, CT, MD, MA, MN, NJ, NM, OR, WA), 3 big states (CA, IL, NY), and the District of Columbia. The bill will take effect when enacted by states with 65 more electoral votes. The bill has passed at least one chamber in 8 additional states with 78 more electoral votes (AR, AZ, ME, MI, NC, NV, OK, VA). A total of 3,705 state legislators from all 50 states have endorsed it.

So this is a trigger law which says when a sufficient amount of states has passed it such that the amount of electoral votes affected adds up to 270 all of the states involved will allot their electoral votes going forward to the winner of the popular vote. When implemented the electoral college is effectively mute and an amendment to eliminate it should be proforma. Enough states with an additional 65 electoral votes are needed to pass the measure.

9. *National Referendum*

A national referendum on "yes or no" questions may be initiated by obtaining verified signatures of 50% of the registered voters in 26 States.

Said referendum will take place at the next scheduled Presidential election on the regular four-year cycle 120 days after qualification is met. Congress shall enact implementing legislation for approved referendum initiatives prior to the next Presidential election.

There are many reasons proposals do not get voted on by congress. Sometimes it is because some other action was not taken to secure the needed support of members of the legislature. Other times it may be because lobbyists paid to protect their own interests defeat a proposal before it could be voted on. These things will never change but it should be possible for the American people to make their wishes known directly to politicians and have those wishes fulfilled without relying on political courage or good will from lawmakers. To fall back on a meme, we can't have nice things because of the professional politicians. Obviously, nothing unconstitutional can be authorized. Questions that are "yes or no" in nature should be put to the people. Proposals for changes in laws and the decriminalization or criminalization of activities can be approved. Implementation of the public opinion would be by formal legislation passed by congress. There is no reason why the voice of the people cannot be heard more directly in our national affairs.

10. Senate Reform

Each State having a population of three million or less shall be represented by two senators. States shall gain an additional senator for each additional three million population increment. The senate will be adjusted after the census every ten years.

The Senate does not provide proportional representation based on population. The result of that quirk is that small population states get a very disproportionate say in legislation and the direction of the country. California has about 39.7 million people in the state, roughly 11.8% of the U.S. population. They are represented by 2 Senators and make up 2% of the Senate. Wyoming has a population of 563.6 thousand people roughly 0.17% of the U.S. population. And yet they get 2 Senators and make up 2% of the Senate. You can go right down the line with

Texas having 29.9 million people and making up roughly 8.7% of the population to North Dakota which has 789.7 thousand people and make up 0.23% of the population. This is the definition of disproportionate representation. Given the power that each individual Senator has, it makes sense to allow more than just 100 people in the country to have that kind of influence. Given our propensity to follow the Romans it should be noted that they started with 300 or so in the Senate but eventually added as many as 600 additional Senators. Truthfully, some of our Senators are pretty much cadavers that get wheeled out when a vote is needed. Why do we assume that only 100 people should be at the highest level of our government, especially if we do not choose those people in a way that respects the will of most of the population. I am not saying that the Senate should be like the House, although a stagnant number of House members should also be looked at. What I do suggest is a filtered system where the number of Senators from a state more closely represents the proportion of that state's population to the country. That along with term limits will ensure new blood and ideas that can work on improving our fragile union. Further, it dispenses with an undemocratic feature of our system and moves us closer to democratic ideals.

11. Reproductive Rights

Access to and use of contraceptive drugs and devices shall not be inhibited or restricted. Abortions may be obtained without restriction up to 20 weeks of pregnancy. After 20 weeks the health of the mother and likely survival and development of the fetus may be justification for termination of the pregnancy.

There is no doubt that sometime between conception and birth a fetus becomes a human being. The trouble (and problem) is that no one knows exactly when that is. No matter how learned or sanctimonious or self-assured they may seem, nobody knows. Some say the fetus is not a person until it draws its first breath outside the womb. That is an extreme position on one side. Others say that from the moment of fertilization the fertilized egg is a person. This is also an extreme position in the other direction. If rapidly dividing and growing cells were the criteria for personhood, then every tumor might be called a person. When the Supreme Court decided Roe vs. Wade, it made a Solomon like decision by introducing the concept of "viability" into the discussion. They recognized the limits of their own understanding and chose this concept as the basis for unrestricted access to abortion. At that time, it was generally thought that viability of the fetus did not occur until 28 weeks. Over time with improvements in technology and medical treatment, it is now thought that viability occurs around 24 weeks. If some cushion is allowed, unrestricted access at 20 weeks or less would seem to be a reasonable compromise until medical science can provide better guidelines. Beyond 20 weeks factors such the life and health of the mother or child should be considered. Most people, except the most fanatical, would be willing to accept an approach that is not extreme in either direction, and allows women to make their own decisions without outside interference. Most of us would be happy never to hear about this subject ever again.

PART TWO

There are other things that do not rise to the level of a constitutional amendment but whose implementation could markedly improve the country and make our lives easier and less contentious. The following are some suggestions for changes in policy, laws and an approach to solving problems that could be beneficial.

1. Taxes and Economy

No one likes to pay taxes, least of all the wealthy. It really doesn't matter if the wealth was inherited or earned. As soon as someone gets money, they are averse to paying taxes. The belief seems to be that they alone can best determine how resources should be spent. Our tax system is progressive meaning the tax burden increases with income. This seems to be based on the idea that "to whom much is given, much is required". The wealthy would argue tat nothing was given to them, they earned it. I can't really argue with that viewpoint. They would also declare that such a system just encourages class warfare and resentment born of envy. Suppose we could construct a tax system that is undeniably fair, simple and easy to comply with, while addressing our altruistic desires such as taking care of low-income persons and families.

I know, people run screaming when a flat tax is proposed but let's see what we can do to overcome the objections and address the concerns. First and foremost, we must stop letting the politicians and lobbyists divide us into tribes then pit us against one another. We treat income as if some are more worthy than others. That is a roadmap to a tangled, contorted system that no one can make sense of. All income will be treated the same no matter how it is derived. This covers wages, salary, rents royalties, commissions, proceeds from sales of any kind, bonuses, inheritance and any other source of income or remuneration. I can hear it now, what about capital, families, and the death tax? Well, the tax rate is a flat 17% with a generous $50000 exemption. This is for each worker independent of marital status or claimed dependents. There are no other deductions. So to answer the concern about families, if a husband and wife both worked each would file a tax return separately and <u>each</u> would get the first $50000 of income free of federal taxes. They would indicate their marital status and identify their spouse. One, not both would list minor children as dependents. That is a lot of support for families. But we are not done. We know the child tax credit can have an immediate and direct effect on reducing child poverty from the early days of the Biden administration. Under this tax system, families making $100000 or less will get a tax credit, paid monthly, for each minor below 18 years of age up to 3 children. Further, any family taking care of an elderly relative 65 years of age or older will get a $5000 tax credit to assist with expenses. Those paid in stock or stock opinions will be taxed at the equivalent monetary value as if they had sold the stock at current market rates. In other words, we never worry about capital gains, we simply pay a transaction fee going in and coming out. Inheritance is taxed as income. Some call this the death tax, which is good marketing but fallacious. The truth is that the one who originally earned the money paid tax on it but the one that inherits it has paid no taxes. To the inheritor it is income. In 2023 the inheritance exemption is $12.93 million. This will be kept, and inheritors will be given 5 years to pay the taxes interest and penalty free. This will allow inheritors of businesses and/or real property to take some time to decide the best course of action and make suitable arrangements. Currently the tax rate on inheritance is from 18%-40% depending on the amount inherited. A flat 17% income tax with current inheritance exemption is an improvement over the current system.

There is one last piece that will tie everything together and reach all economic strata. The minimum wage needs to be raised to $17.50 an hour and indexed to inflation just like social security. Further, anyone working full-time and earning less than $50000 will receive an earned income tax credit to make up the difference. A federal sales tax on all goods and services and financial transactions will be used to generate income lost by the exemptions and tax credits. This includes sales of stock, options, derivatives, and financial instruments of any kind. Those who buy and those who sell pay 15% tax. To address the national debt a national lottery should be instituted with winnings being free of federal and state taxes. States have plenty of experience with lotteries and use the proceeds in many cases to fund education. A national lottery with a minimum payout of $10 million could easily generate $25-$50 million per week. Assuming we stop digging the hole we are in; one can see the light at the end of the tunnel on clearing the debt. After that, what should we do with the money? A national rainy-day fund for catastrophes and unforeseen events would be useful.

Did we come close to doing what we set out to do? First, we wanted to be fair to everyone. In this case we treat everyone the same and everyone pays the same percentage of income. The support for families and children is extensive and much better than what is currently being done. Inheritance is taxed like all other income and the current inheritance exemption is maintained and a generous period is given to pay estate taxes without penalty or interest. That is more than fair. The minimum wage is raised and indexed to inflation to help it keep pace with rising costs. An Earned Income Tax Credit is provided to those making less than $50000 a year to increase their buying power. The lowest income workers have been provided for. This system does not reward certain behaviors or industries. It puts everyone on the same level playing field.

I can hear the complaints now. The charitable industry will say nobody is going to give without deductions. Charitable giving should be done because of compassion and a desire to help, not for tax purposes. Let's give people a chance to show where their hearts are and adjust, if necessary, down the line. The next loud cry will be "too inflationary". The funny thing is that the same amount of spending given in tax cuts for the wealthy or corporations would be considered good investments and sound policy. The US has a 70% or so consumer driven economy. Putting money in the hands of ordinary people means that it will be spent and makes its way through the economy providing needed goods and services as it goes. This purchasing power will create demand and businesses will grow or startups will be created to meet that demand. That sounds like a growing economy to me with jobs increasing.

Additionally, this is a very simple system, and no outside people are needed to help anyone figure out their taxes. If you can do simple math, you can determine your taxes in less than 15 minutes.

Corporate buybacks of their own stock used to be illegal. That practice should be outlawed once again. The practice does not increase market share or grow the business. It is a way to juice the stock price so bonuses can be paid. They say it rewards shareholders, but if they really wanted to reward the shareholder, they would increase dividends or give a special dividend. They say this is not tax efficient. I believe shareholders have the wherewithal to address their own personal tax situation, thank you very much. Buybacks hide corporate weakness and incentivize some managers to take on corporate debt to finance the buybacks. If you want to reward shareholders give them a dividend. Stock should only be purchased to acquire other companies and grow the business or market share.

Note that this proposal mostly deals with personal taxation. Business taxes are left to policy wonks that seek to encourage various types of business activity.

2. Social Security and Medicare

Social Security and Medicare are two of the most successful programs the government has ever implemented. And yet there are those who would weaken or eliminate them if possible. Stil there are some adjustments that need to be made to ensure solvency.

Medicare is relatively easy to address. Until such a time as the US comes to its senses and provides universal health care for its citizens i.e., Medicare for all, the path to solvency lies in removing the income limit for Medicare taxes. The tax rate should be a flat 2.5% on all income for both employee and employer. The age at which the program kicks in is 65. That would not change as health challenges start to manifest in the late 50s and 60s.

Social Security does have a demographic problem in that we are living a lot longer than when the program was originally conceived. We all know we have fewer workers supporting each retiree. It's obvious we need to make some changes to our retirement age. This can be done gradually and with minimum disruption to the plans and lives of current workers. The proposal is to increase the retirement age for someone a year away from retirement by 6.5 weeks. Those workers two years from retirement would add 13 weeks. Those workers that are three years from retirement would add 19.5 weeks and so on. This would continue until the full retirement age is increased to 72 and the early retirement age is increased to 67. The table below shows how workers of various age are affected.

CURRENT AGE	NEW RETIREMENT AGE	EARLY RETIREMENT AGE
67	67	
66	67.125	
65	67.25	
64	67.375	
63	67.5	
62	67.625	62
61	67.75	62.125
60	67.875	62.25
59	68	62.375
58	68.125	62.5
57	68.25	62.625
56	68.375	62.75
55	68.5	62.875
54	68.625	63
53	68.75	63.125

52	68.875	63.25
51	69	63.375
50	69.125	63.5
49	69.25	63.625
48	69.375	63.75
47	69.5	63.875
46	69.625	64
45	69.75	64.125
44	69.875	64.25
43	70	64.375
42	70.125	64.5
41	70.25	64.625
40	70.375	64.75
39	70.5	64.875
38	70.625	65
37	70.75	65.125
36	70.875	65.25
35	71	65.375
34	71.125	65.5
33	71.25	65.625
32	71.375	65.75
31	71.5	65.875
30	71.625	66

29	71.75	66.125
28	71.875	66.25
27	72	66.375
26		66.5
25		66.625
24		66.75
23		66.875
22		67

This change is very gradual and would not disrupt the plans of those close to retirement. Further, the Social Security tax on all income is 7.5% for employees and employers. The funds designated for Social Security and Medicare should be used for nothing else unless a dire emergency such as war is declared. A commission consisting of the Federal Reserve Chairman, Treasury Secretary, the president of the New York Federal Reserve Bank and the Chief Justice of the Supreme Court will oversee the investment of 15% of the proceeds from Social Security and Medicare taxes into index funds such as the S&P 500, Midcap 400 Russell 2000, etc. No investments in individual stocks will be made. This is done to achieve a return that exceeds that of treasury bills and grow the investment. Over time it is hoped that the returns can eliminate the need for any future tax increases. The custodians are chosen because they should have a deep understanding of markets and current conditions and should be able to navigate the markets while protecting the funds. The Chief Justice is chosen primarily to oversee the integrity of the operations and freedom from political considerations.

3. Immigration

Immigration is a complex topic with many aspects that must be addressed. I don't claim to have the solutions to every part of the immigration question. What I do see is that the various sides are dug in, stubborn and sometimes stuck on stupid. Too often groups say if this particular thing isn't done then there can be no progress on any other part of the problem. I suggest a different approach based on the old joke; how do you eat an elephant? Answer, one bite at a time. We should break immigration up into all its constituent parts and focus on solutions for each aspect of the problem. When we think we have a solution that works for one thing, implement it and move on to the next problem. Before you know it as with any big task, immigration will be reduced to a few bite- size, although difficult topics. Obviously, some of the things we must address are border security, millions of undocumented aliens who have lived in the country for years, dreamers, work visas, employers who hire illegals, Immigration courts and lawyers, third country migration drivers. There may be many more issues to be addressed but that is the point. Let's get all our heads together and let's name all the components of the problem and solve each of them based on its own merits.

Concerning border security, I have one fundamental question. Where is the study? We have been talking about border security on our southern border since before the 1980s. Wouldn't you think that sitting on a shelf somewhere collecting dust is a study detailing exactly what must be done at every foot of the southern border. If it exists it should be made public. The study would also address impacts such as water way restriction, animal migration routes, what land can be purchased and what must be taken by imminent domain, access roads, utilities etc. Obviously, barriers make sense in some areas but there will be places where geography precludes the need for anything. Electronic and/or satellite monitoring may be most appropriate in other places. This is step one with border security.

4. Social Justice and Judicial Reform

This country has entirely too many local law enforcement agencies. As a result, these small agencies do not have the resources to maintain state of the art training techniques or best practices in law enforcement. These small organizations should be combined into larger regional agencies that have the manpower and resources to be effective and implement best practices.

A commission should annually review procedures and training practices and focus on judgement, temperament, and integrity in officers. (De-escalation should be the focus of encounters and there should be zero tolerance for misconduct, dishonesty t and unnecessary violence) Institute the following changes:

- Ban Chokeholds and Strangleholds
- Require De-escalation
- If you don't see a gun, don't draw a gun (Use night sticks, tasers and pepper spray)
- Require Warning Before Shooting
- Exhaust All Alternatives Before Shooting
- Duty to Intervene for all officers.
- Ban Shooting at Moving Vehicles
- Detailed Use of Force Procedures and Protocol
- Require Comprehensive Reporting of Misconduct and Illegal Activities
- Dishonesty in Reporting or Charging is Cause for Dismissal
- Suspects shall be restrained with hands at the sides or front of their body.
- Body Cams Shall be Worn by Active Duty Officers in Contact with the Public
- Dash cams are required for all vehicles.

Review DA and Prosecutor actions for similar treatment for suspects with similar offenses and backgrounds. (The whole range of actions from charges filed to plea deals offered and sentences requested should be reviewed for fairness and equity). A day in court before a jury of one's peers is a citizen's right. He should not be penalized for turning down a plea deal in favor of a jury trial by being overcharged or facing extreme sentences that are designed to be coercive but otherwise are unwarranted.

Eliminate for profit bail bondsmen and review amount and need for bail versus electronic monitoring and notification systems for upcoming trials. This can get out of hand, so it requires some common sense in practice. If a person on bail tampers with his tracking device or is charged with another offense, then bail is revoked and they can await trial in jail. Study Scandinavian countries for guidance. (The bail system leads to de-facto debtor's prison for many who are not even convicted of a crime.)

Remove mandatory sentences and study judicial action in delivering similar sentences for similar offenses. (Fairness in sentencing must be part of any overhaul of the justice system. Bad judges need to be removed just like bad police officers.)

De-criminalize possession of all drugs in quantities that indicate personal use intent.

Trials for public officials including police officers must be in front of a jury of their peers from the community they serve. (No more bench trials in front of judges that are close to the public officials where the "fix" could be in before the trail starts.)

5. *Internet and Social Media*

An informed electorate with complete and accurate information will make better decisions for society. Therefore, it should be the goal of information and media regulations to promote and encourage to the maximum extent possible the dissemination of truthful and complete information. The Communications Decency Act, in particular, 47USC230 should be revised with this goal in mind. Below are suggestions for the types of changes needed.

All users of information media accounts must provide complete identity records including name, address, telephone number, email address and government issued photo ID copy to the information technology company for account attribution. Records will be maintained of all active accounts. Organizations such as corporations, partnerships, non-profits, etc. must provide incorporation documents and identities of directors, management, owners, partners etc.

Companies and Platforms engaged in the transmission or post of advertising, news, statements, and assertion of facts online by text, tweet, fax, e-mail, phone, or other methods of electronic transmission shall comply with the Federal Trade Commission (FTC) rules and regulations related to Truth in Advertising and are liable for damages from inaccurate or malicious content. Transmissions and posts shall be fact checked and verified before transmission or dissemination in any form. Opinions must be clearly and distinctively delineated as such and need not be fact checked. Fact checking is required for advertising and news content only. One way to approach this issue is to have the top 10 journalism schools in the country identify the top 10 news organizations based on journalistic integrity and ethics, accuracy, and fairness. If a story appears on the platform of 3 of the chosen news organizations which each has independently verified, it is considered accurate. Other information may be transmitted but with distinguishing marks to categorize it as opinion. Perhaps blue letters on a pink background with a watermark that says OPINION. If readers choose to believe it after the warnings, that is solely on them, and no one is liable for any consequences. The use of AI and physical curators makes this very possible with effort and focus.

Internet search engines shall ONLY prioritize search results based on accuracy, validity, and factual content of results. Steering users to more salacious content is prohibited.

Provisions shall be made to prevent the transmission or re-transmission of content via e-mail, text, tweet, post, fax, phone, or any form of electronic transmission by automated means such as software program, hardware intervention, BOT, or any other non- human individual means. Means shall be provided for users to verify they are not BOTs prior to transmission.

Compliance with this law is the shared responsibility of the content disseminator and the platform or means of distributions. Fines for each violation shall be a maximum of $1000 per user view. Platforms and companies are required to keep statistics on the number of views for each post or transmission.

6. Usury

Usury is mentioned at least 17 times in the Bible. Even Bronze Age scribes recognized the debt trap that high interest rates put individuals in. Why do we allow usury? Are there any reasons interest rates charged should be more than 10 percentage points above the Federal Funds rate charged to banks? Yet when the Federal Funds rate was less than 1% some credit cards were charging 29.9% interest. Individuals that charge such high rates are called loan sharks and are prosecuted. The reason most credit cards come form a few states is that those states have no usury restrictions on interest rates. Why do we allow the American public to be sheared like sheep? We can do better and help our fellow citizens as well as ourselves by limiting interest rates charges.

7. National Oil Company

The US sells leases to oil companies to explore federal lands. The oil beneath those federal lands is the property of the people of the US. Why don't we have our own national oil company and operate more like partners to the companies doing the exploring. Leases would still be awarded for companies to do the exploration. The national company would manage the leases and set priorities for the oil extracted. Why not pay cost plus $10 per barrel for any oil used to fill the Strategic Petroleum Reserve. Why not insist on a discount for oil used in this country and 25% of the profits for oil sold on the world market.

8. The Filibuster, Nominations and Appointments

The current filibuster system allows disingenuous actors to thwart the majority for partisan or petty personal ideological reasons. The Senate should go slower and be more deliberative than the House of Representatives. In the House the minority has very little power. In the Senate the minority must always be heard but not be obstructionist. The following reform will allow the minority to be heard while still allowing a vote and progress to be made.

When a Senator wants to filibuster a bill, appointment, or nomination, it may be done with the assistance of other Senators who are like minded. All Senators must be seated in the chamber to listen to the filibuster. The Senator making the filibuster has 12 hours to make his or her case to their colleagues at which point a 12-hour question and answer period would follow the next day. Again, all Senators are required to be seated in the chamber listening to the discussion. After completion of the questions, a two-week waiting period is held before the bill, appointment, or nomination, is voted on. This is to allow the public to weigh in with their Senators. A vote up or down is then held to resolve the matter. With this system the minority is fully heard and has an opportunity to sway his or her colleges. However, the minority cannot obstruct the majority and prevent progress. If a bad bill is passed, then those responsible will answer to the voters in the next election and if needed the bill can be rescinded.

9. Schools

We need to re-imagine schools. Schools can and should be more than facilities for teaching reading, writing and arithmetic. First, it goes without saying that breakfast and lunch should be offered for all students, It cuts into hunger in this country and positions students to be able to focus and learn more effectively. Parents can be charged based on their ability to pay, and outside organizations can be solicited for assistance to cover costs. There was a public school in New York that noticed several of their students were truant and further that they all lived in the same block. When they investigated further it turned out that the children all lived in the same apartment complex and that the landlord had not paid the water bill and the water to their building had been cut off. The parents would not let their children go to school unwashed with dirty clothes. The school administrators contacted the families and offered to allow them to use the school laundry in the evenings to wash clothes and the school gym to shower and clean up in the morning. The kids all returned to school. Clearly, this was not the school's responsibility, but they saw a problem and a solution that they could offer. This story points the way to what schools could be i.e., a nexus for all needed family and child services. Imagine the school having an administrative office that could put families in contact with any services they might need This would include things like utility assistance, internet connection, rent assistance, food assistance, clothing assistance, shelter assistance, school supplies, mental health counseling, violence counseling, transportation help, job counseling, etc. One stop shopping is where families can connect with agencies and organizations that provide real solutions and help for their problems. There are many organizations, e.g. the foundations of athlete's, that pass out book bags and supplies at the beginning of a school year. Why not have them adopt a school and provide all the materials a school would need for that year, so teachers do not have to come out of pocket to supply materials. Why the schools? They are dispersed throughout communities and families already contact them. They can be a smooth and efficient way to deliver services and meet the people where they are. The services office would not interfere with the administration of the schools or burden teachers. If teachers notice a problem, they would be able to refer the family to the office for services.

Murders and senseless violence plague our communities and is on the rise. Clearly, something is not being communicated to our young people since most of the violence comes from them. There needs to be additional courses taught throughout the school years that instill humanity and compassion into the students. I'm not talking about religious doctrine. But we need to make students look upon their fellow classmates like they do their own brothers and sisters. Further, boys and girls need to interact in such a way that leadership and communications flow frely between the genders. The development of such a curriculum should be by psychologists with input from teachers. Another needed series of classes is parenting. These should be taught from grades 9-12. These are not just budgeting and family economics. Students need to be taught how to raise children and above all how to speak to them in a manner that builds self-esteem and allows the personality to flourish. So many people speak to children in such a harsh manner that it seems soul crushing. It's a wonder we don't have more seria killers running around than we do. We leave parenting to chance and assume young people will learn from their parents and carry on. Something is not happening, and this is too important to be left to chance. I don't know whether our current condition is because of parenting or outside influences. I'm not blaming anyone. We need to do something, and this would be a start. Reading, writing, and arithmetic are not enough to round our students in this modern age.

Resources for public schools must stop being diverted to private and in some cases for profit operations. This is often done under the guise of school choice. Public education is not like shopping for a box of corn flakes where you settle on the store with the best price. Public education is an attempt to educate the masses of the population and better society. The argument is often made about how private schools do things right and the public schools are broken. Well if that is true, why don't we simply do what businesses do when they find their competitors are out performing them in a particular area. Businesses study that competitor, model what he is doing then bring it back and implement it in their own organization. Study the best practices of the top private schools, model them and implement them in the public schools. Some would say the teachers' unions would not allow this. This is a fallacy. Teachers want the absolute best for their students and if the changes are for that purpose and not breaking the union or devaluing the teachers, they will support them.

Vouchers really are about more than education. They are an attempt to starve the public schools of resources and make the taxpayer foot the bill for segregated and religious private schools, or fund unaccountable for-profit institutions.

10. Decriminalize Drug Use

Its time to stop the insanity of waging an unwinnable drug war to prevent people from using substances they want to use while permitting alcohol use along with tobacco use and the myriad of prescription drugs that are available. Addiction should be approached from a public health perspective not a legal one. If anyone wants help with their addiction, it should be provided in as effective a manner as possible. No distinction is made between so called "hard" drugs and "soft" drugs. The suggestion is to treat all "soft "drugs as we do alcohol and use prescriptions for "hard" drugs. The use of prescriptions and government control over quantities dispensed and purity of product will ensure users get what they are seeking in amounts that will not harm them. Further, the tax revenue can pay for the program and provide resources for treatment and rehabilitation. We could save billions on law enforcement efforts and put that money to work in other areas. We would also break the back of the drug cartels and the criminal activity associated with them. We know that Prohibition in the 1920s gave us decades of organized crime families that spread out into all manner of legitimate businesses and drained resources from our communities.

This drug war is no different. We are trying to ban activities that individuals want and will seek out no matter what restrictions we impose. Why not control it and manage the activity to keep it as safe and discreet as possible. Obviously, one could not be underage and the laws regarding driving under the influence or while impaired must be strictly enforced. That aside, why should we care if the neighbors use drugs for recreational purposes on the weekends?

11. Ethics in Politics and the Judiciary

"Sunlight is said to be the best of disinfectants" or so we were told by Louis Brandeis in 1913. Our politicians, judges and executive branch employees should live by a documented code of ethics and be subject to scrutiny by an independent body with the power to investigate and address administratively and/or legally any breaches of the code of conduct. A public corruption division of the Justice Department should oversee reviews for all three branches of government. Further, that division should be proactive and "test" those in public service periodically so that they always understand that someone is watching. This does not prevent various bodies from having their own ethics committees and monitoring and disciplining their own members. It also does not require new rules in all cases. A good starting place is the House Committee on Ethics and its rules with a few adjustments as noted below. We have seen with the Supreme Court that the ethics rules can be weak to non- existent and self-regulation does not work.

Starting with the House ethics rules as a baseline, the following adjustments would be made to enhance the effectiveness of the rules.

A. Members and judges must recuse themselves if they have a direct relationship with those bringing actions or if the immediate family or entity the immediate family works for or with has a relationship with those bringing actions. For the purposes of this rule immediate family covers parents, spouses, children, siblings, cousins, in-laws, nieces, and nephews. The existing rules covers congressional work while this rule is more tailored to judges.

B. Members of the legislative or executive branch or their immediate families may not lobby congress or any part of the federal government for 5 years after completion of service. This also applies to military personnel above the equivalent rank of lieutenant.

C. Members of the federal executive, legislative and judicial branches shall submit their tax returns to the Internal Revenue Service for audit annually in a similar manner as is currently done for the President. Further, returns of these public officials will be public records available to all.

D. No gifts (including services) of value greater than $100 may be accepted without prior written approval. No meals valued at greater than $50 may be accepted.

E. Congressional pensions are abolished in favor of 401K accounts like those of most Americans. Members of Congress can contribute up to 15% of their annual income with the first 5% of annual income being matched dollar for dollar. This would put Congress on an even footing with the public. They watched as the pensions of ordinary people were abolished and now, they should live by the same rules. Besides, it's ridiculous to qualify for a pension after only 5 years.

F. Members of Congress and the judiciary shall not trade stocks directly and may not use confidential information to conduct trades. Blind trusts shall be used to manage all investments while in office overseen by an independent fiduciary trustee.

G. No private meetings with lobbyists. At least two staff members must be present and detailed notes or recordings of all the discussions shall be made. These notes and/or recordings shall be made available to the public via internet within two weeks of the meeting.

H. Attendance at conventions, conferences and meetings must be disclosed.

I. All changes and markups of legislation shall be strictly tracked, and any changes, revisions or markups shall be attributed to the author and all such changes shall accompany the legislation and be made public prior to any vote on said legislation.

J. Judicial nominees shall sign an affidavit agreeing to comply with these rules prior to and as a condition of approval of the nomination. Violation shall be grounds for impeachment.